THE PERSONAL INJURY TRIPOD

What Every Injury Victim Needs to Know

ERIC S. MEYER

Jacobs & Whitehall
9600 Escarpment Blvd
Suite 745-282
Austin, TX 78749
(888) 570-7338
www.jacobsandwhitehall.com

Ordering Information:

Quantity sales. Special discounts are available on quantity purchases by corporations, associations, and others. For details, contact the publisher at the address above.

Orders by U.S. trade bookstores and wholesalers. Please contact Jacobs & Whitehall: Tel: (888) 570-7338 or visit www.jacobsandwhitehall.com.

Printed in the United States of America

Published in 2023

ISBN: 978-1-954506-87-9

Disclaimer

This publication is intended to be used for educational purposes only. No legal advice is being given, and no Attorney-Client relationship is intended to be created by reading this material. The author assumes no liability for any errors or omissions or for how this book or its contents are used or interpreted, or for any consequences resulting directly or indirectly from the use of this book. For legal or any other advice, please consult an experienced attorney or the appropriate expert, who is aware of the specific facts of your case and is knowledgeable in the law in your jurisdiction.

Meyer Injury Lawyers

(833) GO-MEYER

www.meyerinjurylawyers.com

TABLE OF CONTENTS

PREFACE

I wrote this book for people who have been injured through no fault of their own. Insurance companies have made personal injury law a game, and to not be completely taken advantage of, you must know how to play by the rules.

I want people to truly understand what they're getting into when they begin their personal injury case and why their attorney might be doing what they're doing. Unfortunately, attorneys are notoriously bad communicators with their clients, as evidenced by it being the most commonly made complaint to bar exams or bar associations. I want readers in this type of situation to be able to pick up this book, read it, and better understand their situation and the legal process it falls within. Specifically, I hope you come away with an understanding of what is going on throughout the different stages of your case and the importance of retaining an attorney to take lead on your case.

My greatest hope is for your anxiety to be put to rest with the knowledge you take away from this book. Most people go into the personal injury process utterly blind, with no explanation of anything from their attorney. This book is meant to be a little guide to make up for this; a little light, so you don't have to go through your personal injury case in the dark.

DEDICATION

This book is dedicated to every injury victim out there. To all the people whose lives have been changed forever through no fault of their own. To the people who deserve to be paid for their life altering injuries, but due to some heartless insurance company employee who is more concerned about meeting their bonus than they are about making you whole.

Do not lose hope. I truly wish attorneys like me were not needed. I wish insurance companies were honorable. That insurance companies would do the right thing for their customers and pay you what you deserve. Unfortunately, more times than not, they will not. I have been one of them before. I have seen how insurance companies work from the inside. I know their playbook. Hire a good personal injury attorney and fight for your rights.

ACKNOWLEDGEMENTS

There are so many people that have helped me along the way, that there is no way I could list them all here. But, first, I need to say that without the good Lord, none of this would be possible. He has blessed me in many ways. According to Isaiah 40:31, "those who hope in the LORD will renew their strength. They will soar on wings like eagles; they will run and not grow weary; they will walk and not be faint." This verse has been my guiding light.

I also need to thank my beautiful bride, Ashley. You are the love of my life and have been so supportive of me. You truly believe I am the best attorney in the world and your confidence in me motivates me every day. Thank you for everything you have done throughout the years.

I would like to thank all the many mentors and friends who have shaped me along the way. Starting in the early days of law school professors and friends, to those who helped me learn how to navigate my way around the courtroom in the early days. People like Kelly, Susan, Fred, and Jeff. Without your mentorship from the beginning, I would not be anything.

To my dad, Sheldon, and father-in-law, Eric, thank you to both of you for your continued support throughout the years and always taking my calls to answer my questions as I worked up a case. I value both of your advice and I would not be where I am today without either of you.

Also, to my big brother, Mike, you have always been there for me, and I know you always will. We have a bond that few in this world know. Your love and support for me throughout the years means more to me than you will ever know. I love you, bro.

I also need to give a shoutout to my good friends Ryan and Ross. Thank you for your continued help throughout the years. I value both of you as friends and as attorneys. Thank you.

About The Author

The first thing that you should know about me and my practice of the law is that I'm a personal injury lawyer through and through. I *exclusively* handle personal injury cases, but many attorneys that handle personal injury cases do not. This is significant.

My success as a personal injury lawyer really begins as a teen. I have a blue-collar mentality that I bring to a white-collar world. This is because I grew up working on the family farm, working at my friend's ranch, and working various construction jobs. This blue-collar mentality sets me apart from others in my profession.

The journey to becoming a personal injury lawyer traces back to when I was a sheriff's cadet in high school. This is where I fell in love with the law and really found the inspiration that propelled me to eventually become a prosecutor. I eventually went to law school to do just that – become a prosecutor – and while still in law school, I became a certified law student, allowing me to appear in court with supervision.

Even at this stage in my life, I found considerable success before officially starting my career. I stopped counting the number of trials I had at a whopping 150. To be fair, these were not jury trials, but bench trials where people waive their right to a jury. Little did I know that these experiences would lay the foundation for my future as a personal injury attorney.

I continued to build off this foundation once becoming an attorney, something I am proud of and grateful for. After becoming an attorney, I hit the ground running! *Immediately* after being sworn in as an attorney, I walked out of the courtroom and my boss at the time was waiting for me with a case file. He tossed me the documents and said, "Jury selection's in a week. Go have fun." On my first day as an attorney, he threw me out of the boat to see if I would sink or swim. Needless to say, I was ready to swim.

I'll never forget the first day of my first jury trial. I had only been a licensed lawyer for about a week. Before the trial, I was in the bathroom dry heaving, even though I hadn't eaten in three days. My heart raced, my palms were clammy, and I could feel the weight of the courtroom staring at me as I stood before the jury for the first time. I broke through this self-induced pressure about halfway through that first day. At one point, I remember thinking, "I've got this." Since then, I've never looked back.

Over time, as I took on several trials as a prosecutor, my skills and successes caught the attention of a major insurance company in the United States. I was headhunted and became its trial counsel, representing people causing injuries to others in car crashes.

At the time, my wife was working and in law school, and we didn't have any children, so I figured I might as well maximize the time I was working too. In fact, I worked my tail off. This afforded me much trial experience, allowing me to work my way up the corporate ladder. I was the youngest attorney in the company's history to be in the position I was in. I was working on significant cases and representing major corporations. I felt like the main character in my own movie, navigating the complexities of high-stakes litigation to envied success.

Despite this success, I ultimately found myself unfulfilled and burnt out. That's when I made a drastic change and decided to become partners with my wife and start our own practice. Instead of continuing to represent big interests, I started representing victims. I was able to use my experience on the other side to help the people who truly needed it and found so much more fulfillment in it. Today, as a personal injury lawyer, I have handled cases representing people who suffer from minor accidents to those who die wrongful deaths.

It's funny, had you told me while I was in law school that I would eventually become a personal injury lawyer, I would have laughed at you. I remember constantly making fun of civil lawyer, but you truly never know where God will send you. I genuinely believe I am on the path He has for me, doing what I'm supposed to do. I am so grateful and absolutely love what I do. I am very passionate about fighting for my clients and getting them what they deserve. I love helping people and making a difference, and being a personal injury attorney is a way I can do that.

Contrast this with insurance companies and claims adjusters, who essentially work to screw people over, focused only on saving a company money. They have completely stripped the human element out of the process. This infuriates me and was the main reason I left that side. Having been a trial attorney for an insurance company in the past means I learned their playbook. I know their strategies and tactics like the back of my hand. This has given me a unique perspective on how I fight for victims of their game. This is how I beat them to help those who would otherwise be denied being made whole just for others to profit more.

I am married to the love of my life and business partner, Ashley. Together, we have three wonderful children. When I'm not fighting for my clients, you will find me spending time with my family, hunting, fishing, and enjoying the outdoors. I also enjoy helping Ashley run our private school, Freedom Academy.

TESTIMONIALS

Uniquely Qualified To Handle Cases Such As Mine

"Meyer Injury Lawyers does outstanding work! Last year I was broad-sided by another vehicle. The defendant's insurance company attempted to get me to settle for a very low amount. After meeting with Mr. Eric Meyer, I decided that given my medical status, it would be in the best interest of my family and myself to have my case represented by Meyer Injury Lawyers. Eric along with members of his firm went right to work on my case. Their hard work which included negotiating with the defendant's insurance company and my HMO, resulted in me feeling very satisfied with the end result. I believe Eric is uniquely qualified to handle cases such as mine. Prior to going into private practice, he was a successful Deputy District Attorney and he also worked as an attorney for an insurance company. Thank you again Meyer Injury Lawyers!"

– A.L.

****

They Exemplify Caring And Competent Counsel

"Eric and Ashely are a husband and wife super lawyer duo! In my line of work, I deal with many lawyers, so believe me when I tell you they are two of the best out there. My experience with them has been stellar. They exemplify caring and competent counsel, are extremely accessible, and know how to get results."

– C.B.

****

They Develop A Genuine, Personal Relationship With You

"I can't stress enough that the term 'customer service' doesn't apply to them – because they don't have 'customers' or even 'clients' – they develop a genuine, personal relationship with you. They made me feel very at ease and confident that I was receiving expert counsel [...] I happily recommend their services."

– C.S.

****

Makes Us Feel Safe And Confident

"Eric is professional, personal, respectful and awesome. He has always connected with me and my husband in a way that makes us feel safe and confident in trusting him with our needs. I know that the direction and decisions Eric is suggesting are with my husband's, myself and our family's needs in mind."

– L.T.

****

Trust, Integrity, And Respect

"They make you feel like you are the most important client they have ever had, and we all know how important that is these days. Trust, integrity and respect are three words I would use to describe what they represent."

– D.G.H.

****

CHAPTER ONE

FIRST THINGS FIRST

What To Do Immediately Following an Accident

1. Seek Medical Attention

Being involved in an accident can be a terrifying experience, especially if you are visibly injured. Regardless of whether you can immediately discern your injuries, seeking medical attention should be your top priority. Of course, the urgency with which you should seek medical care will depend on your condition, but ensuring your health and physical well-being should be your primary concern.

Don't let fears of medical bills hold you back from getting the treatment you need. If injuries are apparent, seek immediate treatment. If you are uncertain or unable to detect any injuries, get non-emergency medical attention as soon as possible to rule out any unseen injuries that may have occurred. And remember, whatever the type or cost of treatments you undergo, get everything documented and keep all records and receipts related to the accident.

2. Move To a Safe Location

If you were involved in a car crash, and there are no serious injuries, get to a safe location. As much as you want to take photographs of evidence, such as vehicle positions, damage, skid marks, etc.; your safety should be your top priority. Staying in the roadway is not safe. So, if possible, move to a safe location.

3. Call 911

Next, call the police so they can complete a traffic collision report. This traffic collision report (TCR) is a detailed police document that gathers the involved parties' information and, most often determines who is at fault for the accident. If the injuries are serious enough to warrant calling 911, do so. Some police departments do not like taking reports if there are no injuries. If you get met with a roadblock like this, request one to be completed anyway. If 911 is not necessary to come to the scene, you can call the non-emergency line. This will generate a call log/record of the accident in the police department's system to be used as a reference in the future if needed.

4. Gather Information and Take Photos

After calling the appropriate authorities, gathering pertinent information from the other party if you are involved in a motor vehicle accident is essential. Take photographs of their driver's license, car insurance card, and their vehicle registration card. Document other information, such as the other party's phone number and address. Also, take photos of any damage to all the vehicles involved. Additionally, take pictures of the accident scene. Lastly, don't forget to speak to any witnesses, if there are any, and get their name and contact information.

What To Do After a Non-Motor Vehicle Accident

In the case of non-motor vehicle accidents, such as a slip and fall at a grocery store, promptly report the incident to the store manager. This initiates a crucial paper trail for documentation purposes. If the store is equipped with security cameras, make every effort to obtain video footage of the incident as soon as possible. Acting promptly is critical since security camera recordings are typically stored in the cloud and video is overwritten after a certain number of hours. Also, take photographs of the hazardous conditions that caused your slip and fall, such as a puddle, icy surface, or crack in a sidewalk.

Ultimately, remember to try to gather as much evidence as possible at the time of the incident and ensure everything is properly documented. This will make your case go much smoother in the future.

A Note On Engaging With The Other Party

There are some valid reasons to talk to the other party after an incident. First, it is more than appropriate to show concern for their humanity and see if they are okay. Besides this, as noted above, you need to exchange information with them, so ask for it as relevant to your circumstances.

However, when you do talk with them, you have to be very careful not to say anything too revealing. When checking on the other person's status, some people may innocently say something like, "I am sorry to see you hurt." Do not say anything like this. If you do, it can later be construed as incriminating. Using the word *sorry*, in any context, will very likely be used against you. Their attorney or insurance company will likely argue, "Why did you say sorry if you did not cause the accident?"

Beginning The Personal Injury Recovery Process

Whether a motor vehicle accident, trip and fall, dog bite, or a defective product injured you, you need to call a personal injury attorney as soon as possible. This will get things moving off the bat. They will then take things over for you and ensure your case moves in the right direction and speed. Often, if you have not already done so, the first thing your attorney will do is file claims with the insurance companies involved. If, for whatever reason, it is unclear whether the other party has insurance, there are ways that a proper personal injury attorney can find out how to proceed.

When it comes to filing a claim with your own insurance company, it is important to note that your policy is essentially a contract. Specific clauses in the contract require that you cooperate with the company, meaning you must file a claim with your own insurance company. Filing a claim with your own insurance company does not impact your policy and premium, if you are not at fault. For simplicity's sake and for a stronger case, you should retain an attorney as soon as possible and have them do it on your behalf. If you do not retain an attorney, be sure to file the claim immediately – but keep in mind that anything you disclose to your own insurance company can possibly come back and haunt you later in your case.

If the other party has insurance, chances are they will also report the accident to their insurance company. When they do, a claims representative will most likely contact you within a couple of hours or days after the accident. When the representative calls, do not talk to them about your claim. Tell them you have retained an attorney, then provide your attorney's name and contact information. Alternatively, if you do not have a personal injury attorney, simply tell the adjuster that you do not want to talk to them. Remember: adjusters will twist whatever you say to use against you. It's best to avoid the situation entirely. There is no law requiring you to speak with a claims representative at this point in the process – don't shoot yourself in the foot by saying something you will later regret.

A Warning About Early Settlement Offers

Insurance companies often offer settlements promptly after a claim is filed. Do not be fooled! These are just thinly-veiled attempts to make your claim disappear at a fraction of its worth. When you accept a settlement offer, you will have to sign a release. Doing so is entering into a binding contract wherein you agree not to go after the insurance company for any more money after that date. This is legally binding even if your injuries later end up being worse than you originally thought and are proven to be the result of the incident in question. If your neck pain doesn't go away or you develop new symptoms a few months after the incident, you'll be left with absolutely no recourse.

In fact, I just recently wrapped up a case where the insurance company offered my client a settlement right off the bat. My client had been trying to resolve the case on their own, but she was getting increasingly frustrated with the process. It was at this point that she retained me, and I worked up the case - getting her over four times the money that the insurance company initially offered her.

This story highlights the little-known truth: that insurance companies make money in two main ways. The first method is obvious, people sign up for policies and pay premiums. The second method is less clear, they make money by taking advantage of people and underpaying on claims. As tempting as it may be, never take a settlement offer upfront without the guidance of a genuine personal injury attorney. If you do not have a personal injury attorney in your corner, you will be taken advantage of.

One of the most prevalent misconceptions I have encountered throughout my years as a personal injury attorney is the belief that the process is easy and that insurance companies are actually there to help. Insurance companies want you to believe this, but nothing could be further from reality. Insurance companies are ultimately profit-driven corporations. Insurance companies are not your friend, nor do they exist to help you. They are your enemy.

CHAPTER TWO

THE PERSONAL INJURY TRIPOD

Whether sitting in a consultation with a new client or working up an existing client's case, I explain that personal injury is like a tripod. If you take away one leg from a tripod, it will not be able to stand. Likewise, there are three essential "legs" to every personal injury claim: liability, damages, and money. Just like a tripod, if you take one of these essential "legs" away, the case will fall over.

Liability

As the injured party, you have to prove that the other person did something wrong. You can have the worst injury imaginable, and the other person can have the most excellent insurance - but if you caused the accident, there's no liability. If there is no liability, there are no grounds to seek compensation from the other party.

Negligence is the most common form of liability. This occurs when someone is legally obligated to do or not to do something, but has breached that duty. For example, you have a duty to drive safely and obey the rules of the road, but you can be held liable for damages if you breach that duty of safety and rear-end the person in front of you. Alternatively, if you sue someone in a premises liability claim, it would be based on the negligent maintenance of their property.

Other cases have strict liability, meaning you do not even have to prove that the person neglected to uphold their obligation - they are liable simply by virtue of the incident happening. Examples of this include dog bite claims, where if a person's dog bites someone else, they are held strictly liable. Similarly, when injured while using a product, the company can be held strictly liable for the product being defective.

Damages

Some car accident cases can remind you of scenes from an action movie, with cars flipping as explosions light up the sky in the background. Some are much simpler, yet still cause damage. If someone isn't injured, there's no personal injury case. When the *damage* leg to the personal injury tripod is cut out, the tripod falls over.

Like liability, there are several types of damages. The first type of damage that you can readily calculate, is ***special damages***. Medical bills are a great example of this since they are easily quantifiable. You can argue to the other party, "My medical bills were $65,000, so I'm suing you for $65,000." or "I make $35 an hour and missed 1,000 hours of work, so I'm suing you for $35,000."

The next type of damage is ***general damages***. These are not strictly calculable, but rather account for the pain, suffering, inconvenience, and embarrassment you experience due to an incident. When calculating general damages, you have to have an experienced personal injury attorney who knows the value of this aspect of your case, as many variables will come into play. Proving these damages often requires hiring experts who can provide relevant insight, estimates, and advice regarding medical treatment that might not be obvious in the short term to non-medical professionals.

Lastly, is ***punitive damages,*** that are intended to act as a means of financially punishing the other party for their actions. Punitive damages are rarely sought after in personal injury cases because the defendant's conduct must be egregious in order to seek them.

Money

You probably know the commonly quoted line from *Jerry Maguire,* "Show me the money!" It's very relevant here! There has to be some amount of money involved in a personal injury case. You could be involved in a car accident with clear liability where you get rear-ended by someone on the freeway with glaring injuries, but if there's no money to pay for those injuries, the personal injury tripod is no tripod at all – it's a sad, tipped-over duopod. It is a sad reality, but a person's injuries and even a person's life, can be valued simply by how much insurance the other person has.

I am currently handling a case where a gentleman was driving down the freeway, was rear-ended, and killed. There is clear liability and damages, but the person who hit him was uninsured, doesn't have any personal assets, and my client does not have uninsured motorist coverage, so there's no way to acquire money. Unfortunately, the tripod collapsed in this case. It broke my heart, but this case is an excellent example of why insurance is the center of so many of the legalities surrounding personal injury cases.

Due to the high amount of funds required to cover an injured person's damages, you typically need to obtain money from an insurance company, not directly from the other party. In some cases, you can go above and beyond the insurance limits and attempt to strike at personal assets, but the insurance money is generally the surest bet of actual recovery. There are also strategies and tactics that a good personal injury lawyer can use to potentially recover more than the policy limits from the insurance company. These strategies and tactics are very nuanced, though, and you NEED to have an experienced personal injury lawyer for this to happen.

In today's society, with so many living off of credit or paycheck to paycheck, the insurance limits that someone carries often determine a case's value. For instance, in California, the minimum limit for insurance is $15,000. Hypothetically, if you were to get in a car accident with someone with only $15,000 of insurance and require spine surgery as a result, as per the contract, the insurance company party only has to pay $15,000. Anything above and beyond this amount would have to be paid directly by the other party. Of course, most people do not have the means to pay for these damages, nor do they have any valuable assets to go after. As disheartening as it is, the unfortunate reality is that the value of a life in these cases is only as much as the person has in insurance coverage.

This is why many attorneys say, "You can't squeeze blood out of a turnip." Simply put, if the person that caused the accident doesn't have any valuable assets of their own, you can squeeze them all you want, but you won't get any money out – because it's just not there. Fortunately, there are ways of "popping" an insurance policy in some cases, forcing it to pay above and beyond the policy limits that the person is carrying. But to do this successfully, you need an outstanding attorney who can work the case in such a way that, by law, the insurance company will have to pay more than the policy is worth.

CHAPTER THREE

DETERMINING THE VALUE OF A CASE

The ultimate question that every client wants to know the answer to is, "how much is my case worth?" A lot of factors come into play when determining the value of a case. Trying to determine the value of a case may seem like trying to throw darts with a blind fold on, but a good personal injury attorney uses his or her experience to come up with a valuation.

The first factor to take into consideration is good attorneys will begin by asking some simple questions that may take some time to answer, such as how much in special damages the case contains. For instance: Are several thousand or several hundreds of thousands in medical bills under consideration? Will they need future care? How much? What will it cost? Has the victim lost income as a result of the incident? Will they need to take time off work in the future? Will their income suffer? Will their career trajectory be significantly affected?

These questions don't even begin to consider general damages, such as: How much pain and suffering did the victim suffer? How much pain and suffering are they likely to suffer in the future? Do they suffer PTSD because of the accident? What is the prognosis for them because of their injuries? How have the injuries affected the victim? Are they unable to take care of or play with their children now? Are they unable to participate in their hobbies now? If, for instance, someone is an avid golfer and they cannot swing a golf club anymore, that has significant value, and the victim needs to be adequately compensated.

Another consideration when determining the value of a case is the venue, or which court the case will be handled is located. Is the venue conservative or liberal? Generally speaking, jurors from liberal jurisdictions will award higher amounts of money than conservative ones. As a result, you can take the same case to two different counties, and it will come out with two different values. Even if a case is settling prior to a jury trial, a lot of value depends on what you think you can get awarded from a jury and what your chances of getting that amount are.

Beyond these concerns is the quality of the evidence. Are there any independent witnesses? Photographs? Surveillance video footage? I am currently handling a case where my client was involved in a head-on collision. Fortunately for him, he had a dash cam in his vehicle. It is one thing to simply talk about how the other party crossed the solid double yellow lines, but when a jury watches actual video footage, there is a good chance the value of that case will explode because of the "wow factor" the footage brings.

Like evidence, the quality of the injured person and the defendant in the case is crucial. I hate saying this, but the unfortunate reality is that personality plays into so much in the judicial system. Whether a jury likes you or not can considerably weigh in on a case's outcome. In fact, when I worked as an attorney representing insurance companies, I would schedule a deposition so I could interview the injured person and witnesses. After every deposition, I would write a report for the insurance company. In my report, the first thing I wrote about had nothing to do with how the person got hurt, what their injuries are, or what treatment they had received. It instead was about personality and what kind of witness will the person make. Will the jury like them or not? Sympathize with them? Will a jury believe them? I focused on this aspect first because that is how important it is.

Finally, a massively consequential factor determining the value of any case is the quality of the attorneys. Is the defense attorney an A-plus attorney? Is the plaintiff's attorney an A-plus attorney? What kind of grade would you give that attorney? Because that obviously matters.

I cannot tell you how many times I have been asked what a case might be worth. While an attorney can help give you an estimate of what the case's value may look like, you never know until you decide to accept a settlement offer or a final judgment is made. Some people are more risk adverse than others and would rather settle for a guaranteed amount, as opposed to someone who is more willing to go to trial. At the end of the day, though, the bottom line is this: there are countless variables that come into play when estimating the value of a case and no two cases are the same.

Insurance Companies' Tactics

There are a lot of tactics insurance companies use to devalue a solid case. Fortunately, I am very well versed in these tactics because of my experience on the inside of an insurance company. This gives me both a unique approach *and the upper hand.* The first time I speak to a potential client, I look at their case through the lens of what it might look like at trial and what defenses are likely to be used by the insurance company. I firmly believe one of my strengths is to be able to look at things objectively, analyze them deeply, and weigh the strengths and weaknesses.

One of the most common tactics insurance companies use is to skew ***comparative negligence***. Under comparative negligence rules, the injured person can be partly at fault for an accident and the value of their case is diminished by that percentage of fault. Insurance companies employ this tactic for one purpose only: to drive down the value of the case and pay you less. Let's say a case is worth $100,000, and the injured person is found to be 50% at fault. By the rules of comparative negligence, the $100,000 claim would be reduced by 50%, making the case worth only $50,000. Insurance companies use this tactic on thousands upon thousands of claims throughout the country – and save millions upon millions of dollars as a result.

Insurance companies also frequently argue that ***an injury was preexisting***. For example, most people have issues with their necks, be it genetic, prior injuries, or from hunching forward constantly looking at a computer or smartphone. If a person suffers a neck injury, an insurance company may try to claim that the neck injury wasn't caused by the accident at all, but that it was present already beforehand. Of course, a genuine personal injury attorney will know how to counter this argument. When it comes to preexisting injuries, for instance, a lot of times, the "normal" wear and tear you have is asymptomatic, meaning you don't experience any symptoms, but the force of an incident such as a slip and fall or a car accident will cause it to become symptomatic. The law is very clear that if a defendant makes a preexisting injury worse, they are on the hook for it.

Another defense I see often is the argument that the incident had a ***lack of sufficient force*** to cause the injury. I am about to begin a jury trial for a case where my client was involved in a motor vehicle accident. She was rear-ended, and it was a very minor impact, but after that accident, she began to display symptoms of having a traumatic brain injury. Her symptoms persist, to her detriment. In this case, the defense will likely argue that the impact was not sufficient enough to cause a brain injury, but I, in addition to her doctors, believe they are wrong. The insurance company is hiring all kinds of experts like accident reconstructionist, biomechanical engineers, and neurologists. They will likely present nothing more than what I refer to as *junk science*. Because of this, I am taking the case to a jury trial to force this insurance company to pay what my client rightfully deserves.

Another tactic frequently exploited by insurance companies is the different ***caps on damages*** that some states have. For instance, in California, if you have a medical malpractice case, there is a certain limit to what a person is permitted to recover for their pain and suffering. In Idaho, this is true for *all* injury cases. However, sometimes there are ways around these caps, and an excellent personal injury attorney can make it happen.

Recovering After An Accident With An Uninsured Or Underinsured Driver

Being in a car accident is a nightmare to begin with! Even more so if the other party doesn't have adequate insurance, or worse, no insurance at all. However, this does not mean you cannot get any compensation. Uninsured and underinsured motorist coverages are designed to mitigate this risk. Underinsured motorist coverage applies when the person that caused the accident has a small policy that would not cover all the damages you suffered. With underinsured motorist coverage, you can go after your own insurance policy to get the balance of what your case is worth. In addition, uninsured motorist coverage applies when the person that caused the accident has no insurance at all. In this instance, your own insurance policy covers all the damage you suffered.

These coverages are vital and I encourage everyone reading this book to look into your insurance company's offerings for these protections and update your current policy after doing so. I cannot count how many times I have sat down with clients and told them I could not get them more money because the other person either didn't have insurance or was underinsured with only minimum policy limits, and my client did not have sufficient coverage. The truth is, most people simply do not have enough coverage. Not only are underinsured and uninsured motorist coverages extremely affordable, it can make a massive difference if you ever need it.

CHAPTER FOUR

RECEIVING MEDICAL CARE DURING THE CLAIMS PROCESS

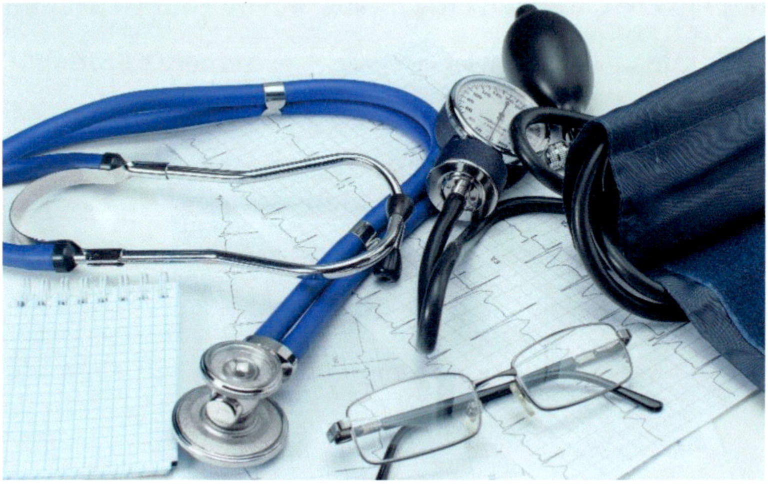

After you initially file a personal injury claim, the case enters what I refer to as "the evidence gathering phase". During this phase, the focus is on making sure that the injured person receives all the medical care they need and starting the recovery process. This is primarily a waiting game to allow for you to heal. It can feel like a long time or an unfortunate reality for most people, but it is critical, because it's the only way to determine the full scope of your injuries, the associated costs of care, and thus the value of the overall case.

Once a general sense of the scope of the case's value is known because the injured person is medically stationary, your personal injury attorney will compile all the evidence and he or she may send a demand letter. These letters provide an analysis of the case and offer a settlement based on what is demonstrated by the evidence. The insurance company will then answer the letter with a counteroffer, which initiates the negotiation phase. If this phase proves unsuccessful, the case moves to litigation.

Personally, I don't wait until my client is medically stationary to get the ball rolling. I start getting to work early in the evidence gathering phase. I guide clients through the process of getting necessary medical treatment, answering all their questions and making suggestions that may benefit their case. I also work ahead of time to gather all the evidence I will need later in the process, including traffic collision reports, expert opinions, and copies of medical records.

A case that I recently settled very clearly exhibits this. The highest settlement offer amounted to $75,000 prior to litigation, but I knew there was more to the case and fought for few years. Over the course of three years, my client wanted to settle multiple times, yet I encouraged him to hold out because I knew by waiting, he would continue getting the medical treatment he needed, which would only drive up the value of the case. A couple of days before the trial, the opposition offered a million dollars out of the blue! I advised my client to take it, and they happily did.

Interacting With Medical Professionals

Getting medical treatment as soon as possible isn't just good for your health, it's vital to increasing your chances of success, both during the evidence gathering phase and in the final outcome as well. Cases so often live and die by medical records – especially the things that are left out of those records are frequently what come back to haunt people in the future. In order to get the best outcome, it's best to take a proactive approach and advocate for yourself. Whenever you speak with medical care providers, be it a nurse, the doctor at the hospital on the day of the injury, or even your primary care physician, be ready to explain your injuries and symptoms in clear detail. And remember, when you do get treatment, make sure it is thoroughly documented.

Additionally, do your best not to say anything dismissive, incriminating, or dishonest, as it can come back and weaken or destroy your case. I have seen countless instances of clients not telling their doctor they were experiencing a symptom or explaining it away. Unfortunately, many people even fail to realize an injury to one part of the body can cause pain and injury elsewhere. Spine injuries are a strong example of this, as they can cause fingers, hands, feet, and toes to go numb. I have had clients tell me that they did not tell their doctor about symptoms because they did not know they were related to each other. In order for medical professionals to adequately understand your symptoms and better develop your treatment plan, it is important to be as specific as possible in identifying, recording, and explaining your symptoms.

My best advice? "Scan" your body from your head down to your toes and take note of any pain, discomfort, numbness, or tingling - any symptoms at all. Log your symptoms in a journal, so to take these notes with you when you see a doctor, as chances are you will forget some of them. On top of this, sometimes the seemingly least consequential symptom can end up being the most significant aspect of the case. Omitting it from medical records can sink your ship!

Getting A Second Opinion

Many fail to realize that they can seek medical care apart from their primary doctors, as they please. In this sense, you can think of a doctor as you would a mechanic: if you have issues with your vehicle and you take it to a mechanic, you are not obligated to have that mechanic perform the work they deem necessary. Instead, you might choose to take your car to another mechanic for a second opinion. Why wouldn't you do the same for your own body?

I am reminded of a client I had. When getting ready for trial, she did not like the advice her primary care gave her, so she asked me if I knew any other doctors that could give her a second opinion. She decided to seek treatment with that doctor and they are now overseeing and coordinating all aspects of her treatment.

The Importance Of Consistency

I cannot stress enough how important it is to get medical care and avoid any gaps in treatment. You need to get the medical care you need and deserve. Unfortunately, to a certain extent, you must be your own proactive advocate in getting that care. Meaning, that it is extremely important that you make time to call medical providers, schedule and go to the appointments on a regular basis. Do not solely rely on medical providers to contact you. If you fail to be proactive with your treatment, this creates gaps in your treatment. The insurance companies will argue that you are not truly injured. The insurance companies will assert that, "Injured people get treatment!" and, "They clearly suffered a subsequent injury that has made the other injury worse. That is why they're here, and they simply don't want to admit that." So, get the treatment you need, and get it often.

Follow the doctor's instructions without a trace of deviation. If the doctor says go to physical therapy, go to physical therapy. If the physical therapist says do home exercises, do the home exercises. This way, you can go in front of a jury and testify that, to the best of your knowledge, you did everything instructed and possible to get better.

Charts, graphs, and calendars are commonly used in the courtroom during a trial. The calendars often mark dates of appointments or conversations with your doctors. Too often, I'll follow up with a client to see if they have scheduled an MRI they were told to get by their doctor. "Well, the imaging facility was supposed to call me, but they haven't yet," they'll reply dismissively.

"That was three months ago," I remind them. "Have you called them?"

"No, not yet," they'll admit. Allowing this to happen and having a judge or jury visualize it in the courtroom doesn't do your case any good at all. Remember: to get the best outcome, you must be proactive.

Paying For Medical Bills While Waiting For A Settlement

A massively common misconception people have regarding personal injury cases is that the other person's insurance company will pay for their medical bills as they wait for the conclusion of their case. Unfortunately, this is just not true. In reality, you will be responsible to pay for your medical bills throughout the duration of your case. This might strike a sense of fear in you, but it doesn't necessarily have to be as harsh as it may seem. In fact, this can work in various ways.

1. **Health Insurance**

The most common way of handling medical expenses is paying it on your own, as if it were not the result of someone else's negligence, through your own health insurance. Under this method, you'd go to the doctor, give them your health insurance card, and they would directly bill your insurance as though it were just a normal injury or disease you were treated for. If you have a copay or a deductible, you would have to pay for that out of pocket. In your personal injury case, you would keep the receipts of all copays and deductibles paid, to include these expenses in the damages, meaning you would be reimbursed. Most of the time you will have to reimburse your health insurance company out of the settlement or judgement. This area of law can be very complex, and a good personal injury attorney will know how to negotiate and reduce these bills.

2. Medical Liens

A medical lien allows a patient to enter into a contract with a doctor who agrees not to require payment for the treatment until the case concludes. Under this system, any treatment received under a medical lien and bills accrued for services, will be paid at the end of the case from the settlement. Many doctors don't like this system because they don't want to wait for their money, while others will have no problem entering into this agreement with you. Fortunately, some attorneys (including myself) have connections with chiropractors, physical therapists, pain management physicians, and surgeons that can perform expensive treatments with patients on a lien basis.

3. **Med Pay Coverage**

Many people have the option to bill their med pay coverage. This is a portion of your own auto insurance policy allotted to cover medical bills. It is not uncommon for clients to have this coverage on their auto insurance policy, and not even know it. Simply, it is having a health insurance policy included with your auto insurance policy.

4. **Funding Companies**

There are companies that will fund medical treatment for you during the claims process. Through this method, you enter into a contract with a company who will pay for your medical treatment. This is similar to how a health insurance company would pay for your medical treatment and you agree to pay them back when your case ends.

Post-Settlement & Post-Judgment Health Insurance Reimbursement

When your health insurance company covers your medical treatment, you may be obligated to reimburse them depending on the terms of your policy. The repayment amount varies, and it's crucial to understand whether it's a dollar-for-dollar reimbursement or a lesser amount. This is because health insurance companies operate based on contractual agreements, and the type of insurance policy you have can significantly impact your obligations.

Most people are unaware of the various types of health insurance policies beyond HMO or PPO, such as ERISA plans, self-insured plans, and capitated insurance plans. Unfortunately, the complexities involved in these plan contracts can significantly affect your reimbursement requirements. Furthermore, if you have government entities (such as Medicare, Medicaid, or the VA) involved, you must follow unique procedures that can be even more complicated and intricate. Knowing how to handle these claims and reimbursements in these instances is essential, as failure to do so correctly can result in serious legal problems. This is yet another reason why seeking out the help of an experienced personal injury attorney is so critical.

CHAPTER FIVE

GETTING THE COURT INVOLVED

If the case cannot be resolve between yourself and the other party or their insurance company, you get the court system involved. This is essentially what is meant by the term "litigation." It is the process of filing a lawsuit against the other party. In the United States, you have a constitutional right to go to trial with a jury. Alternatively, you can choose to waive these rights and appear before a judge without a jury present. With few exceptions, I advise my clients never to waive their right to have a jury present in their trial.

The Statute Of Limitations

The statute of limitations refers to how long you have to file a lawsuit. The statute of limitations for personal injury cases varies by state. In California and Idaho, (the states I currently practice and have offices in) victims have two years from the date of the injury to file their lawsuit. However, like so many other things in law, there are exceptions. For this reason, I highly recommend seeking guidance from a qualified personal injury attorney, particularly in situations where information carries significant implications for your life.

For example, in Idaho and California, the statute of limitations varies for minors and individuals filing lawsuits against government entities. When suing government entities, the time limit may be reduced from two years to six months, wherein you have to file certain paperwork with the involved government entity. Additionally, there may be additional steps to follow beyond those required in a standard personal injury lawsuit.

The Venue

The venue, or the court in which the case is filed, plays a huge factor when determining the value of a case. You can take the same case to two different counties, and it can come out with two different values. If you have an option as to where the venue will be, choose the county where you think you can get the most amount in compensation.

Generally speaking, you have the option of filing a lawsuit either where the incident occurred or in the county where the defendant(s) lives. In many cases, the parties will live in the same county where the incident occurred. In these instances, the venue is limited to that county. But if the incident involved someone from another county or state, the venue could be that location. Additionally, there are times when you can file in federal court as opposed to state court.

Attorneys, Court Fees & Other Case Expenses

Many people have the misconception that they cannot afford an attorney, or the costs associated with litigation. However, this is not true. As discussed in more detail in the next chapter, almost all personal injury attorneys set their fee structure up by taking a percentage of the settlement or judgement when the case concludes. Attorneys are actually the ones who typically cover the expenses of the case. These expenses can range from a few hundred dollars to hundreds of thousands of dollars, depending on the complexity and scale of the case. This is a "contingency fee", meaning that you do not pay for anything up front. Regardless of the amount, the attorney will bear the expenses and be reimbursed at the end of the case. Nothing comes out of your pocket.

Once A Case Is Filed

Once a case is filed, it enters the litigation stage. Litigation consists of several phases, the first of which is the ***pleading*** phase. After you file a complaint, the other party will file a responsive pleading, most often an answer to the lawsuit. These answers typically consist of denials of everything in the complaint. Some of my clients get frustrated because these answers are often so completely absurd, denying that their client had ever been at the scene or involved in the incident at all. Despite the absurdity, I reassure my clients that it is an ordinary and legally legitimate course of action for them to take.

Moving beyond sorting out the pleadings, your case enters the next phase of litigation, the ***discovery*** process. Typically speaking, the first step of discovery includes written interrogatories. These are written questions sent back and forth between the two parties, with usually 30 days to respond under the penalty of perjury. These questions range from asking you to state your name, date of birth, how the incident happened, how you were injured, what your injuries are, where your medical treatment was done, how much it cost, where you work, and whether you lost any income. Additionally, attorneys often hire experts during the discovery phase. Experts are critical to personal injury cases as they are able to look at all the evidence and give informed opinions on what it means or implies.

A Note About Experts

There are two different types of experts: ***non-retained experts*** and ***retained experts***.

- ***Non-retained experts*** are experts that an attorney does not hire to give an opinion on the case yet will still testify. The most common non-retained experts in personal injury cases are the doctors who treat victims. The doctor will typically testify about the nature of the injuries, the prescribed treatment, and why that treatment was necessary.
- ***Retained experts*** are experts that an attorney retains, or hires, to provide their opinion relevant to a case. There are many types of retained experts, including doctors, accident reconstructionists, biomechanical engineers, mechanical engineers, experts on building codes, and more.

Personally, I often hire experts before I ever even file a litigation case. For example, if I have a client who suffered due to a defective product, my first phone call is to an expert on the product.

Next, is the ***deposition*** phase. A deposition is the time for attorneys to talk to witnesses and find out what they know. It is a question-and-answer session that is held under the penalty of perjury. As the plaintiff or injured party in the case, you are a witness, so you will typically be the first to be deposed. (Technically, you could take depositions before written interrogatories, but they typically follow them.) Additionally, ***medical exams*** are often completed during this part of the process, allowing insurance companies to have a doctor that they have hired complete a medical examination on the injured party. While some states require insurance companies to provide a reason for why they should be allowed to conduct these exams, other states give insurance companies full permission to request these exams without needing to provide an argument as to why they are necessary.

If settlement negotiations do not prove fruitful up to this point, your attorney may seek a resolution through ***mediation***. Mediation involves both parties coming together with a neutral third party, often another mediating attorney who has no prior involvement in the case. The mediator then facilitates discussions between the parties and works toward finding a resolution for the case. Finally, if all efforts have been exhausted and you are still unable to obtain a favorable settlement offer, your case will ultimately go to ***trial***.

Uninsured/Underinsured Motorists Claims & Required Arbitration

In an uninsured motorist or underinsured motorist action, your ability to file a lawsuit and have your case heard in a courthouse depends on the laws of the state you are in. In California, for instance, virtually every insurance company includes clauses in their contracts that stipulate if you have a dispute regarding the uninsured or underinsured motorist clauses of your policy, you are required to waive your right to a trial and instead participate in arbitration. Arbitration is similar to a lawsuit in a courthouse but differs in that the two parties agree on hiring an arbitrator, or a neutral attorney, who acts as a judge. It is typically much more relaxed than proper litigation.

A Word To The Wise: Steer Clear Of Pre-Settlement Funding

Pre-settlement funding companies flood TVs across the U.S. with commercials promising an advance on your settlement money if you're in litigation. I've had clients use these services against my advice. I discourage my clients, and everyone reading this book, from signing on with one of these companies. Why? Their interest rates are astronomically high, meaning you collect much less money in the end. Besides this, it also slows down your case's settlement because another entity is involved in it.

CHAPTER SIX

HOW TO CHOOSE THE RIGHT PERSONAL INJURY ATTORNEY

The Power Of A Personal Injury Attorney

Having an attorney by your side when you're going through the personal injury process is absolutely vital. As I mentioned earlier in the book, insurance companies have turned personal injury claims into a game - and you need to know how to play the game in order to win. An excellent personal injury attorney knows the game like the back of their hand.

On top of this, personal injury law is intrinsically one of the most complicated areas of law. Attorneys not only have to know the law pertaining to injuries and damages, but also insurance law, the evidence code, and the code of civil procedure. In order to be even more effective, they must have a strong sense of the medical aspects of injuries as well.

As an example, let's say you were involved in a car accident and suffered a spine injury as a result. Your attorney would need to know all about the spine, understand the basics of herniated discs, how the nervous system works, what medical procedures will be done, what those medical procedures are like, and whether they are simple injections or complicated surgical procedures. If you do in fact require surgery, your attorney will even need to know both *what type* of surgery it is and *how* it will be done. *Why?* To effectively cross-examine doctors.

Many attorneys say they can handle personal injury cases, but they are not genuine litigators - and this key difference can profoundly affect the outcome of a case. Proper trial attorneys tend to win much more money than those who are not effective at arguing a case in court because insurance companies keep note of attorneys that are willing to go to trial (and tend to win). How do I know this? Because I used to be on that team, so I know more than just the rules of their game – I know their strategies and weaknesses too.

Finding The Right Attorney

When searching for a personal injury attorney, the most important things to consider are their experience and what kind of law they practice. Many attorneys are strictly personal injury attorneys, but they're not litigators or trial attorneys. They're very good at working up a case toward a settlement in pre-litigation. They have implemented systems and operating procedures in their practice to get your medical records quickly in an attempt to find a swift resolution, but they won't go to court and fight for you. Because of that, insurance companies will take advantage of them as well.

I am a third generation attorney; I know the legal industry well. Many attorneys out there are *general practitioners*. Think of a primary care physician in the medical world: you go to them for pretty much anything, but they eventually refer you to a specialist if you have an issue that requires attention beyond their abilities. A personal injury attorney is a specialist, like a cardiologist or a neurologist, who focuses their entire career on one specific area of the law.

So, to get a sense of what a prospective attorney is like and how they will be able to deliver value, you need to find out if they are a *genuine* personal injury attorney. Inquire as to whether they handle cases in other areas of law. The best personal injury attorneys practice personal injury law exclusively. Take this story for example…

A nearby general practitioner working on a personal injury case called me a while back, telling me, "I've got a case I'm working on that I'd like to refer to you. I have a settlement in place, but I just realized the person that caused the accident was working at the time and his employer used to be a client of mine, so I have a conflict of interest," he explained. "Can you just wrap up the settlement for me?"

"Sure thing," I answered. But after reviewing the file, I called him back. "What are you doing settling this case for that amount?" I asked with unease.

"That's all it's worth," he replied. I could almost hear him shrugging over the phone.

"What do you mean?" I asked. "This case is worth way more than that."

The attorney explained that the client had gotten better… or so he thought. The truth was, even though the client was saying that her injuries had healed, because of the knowledge I'd acquired over years of handling injury claims, I knew that she would need another surgery in the future. I discussed the intricacies of the medical side of the case with the other attorney and he agreed that I should put the settlement on hold. Sure enough, a few months later, the client was scheduled for surgery, and I ended up settling the case for almost *seven times* the amount that they nearly walked away with.

Don't mistake my purpose of telling this story for a lack of humility or respect for my colleague, he is a fantastic litigating attorney. To this day, I call him for advice on strategy for certain things. But I do not ask him for advice on personal injury cases because he is not a *genuine* personal injury attorney.

The Truth About "Affording" An Expensive Attorney

Many have the misconception that there is no way they can afford a personal injury attorney. Contrary to that belief, this simply is not true. All the genuine personal injury attorneys I know do not charge an hourly fee. Instead, they charge a contingency fee. Under this payment structure, you do not have to pay your attorney anything up front, nor do you have to pay a retainer agreement. The attorney takes a percentage of the awarded fees upon the conclusion of the case.

The percentage varies from attorney to attorney and is based on both what stage the case is at and whether it settles or goes to trial. Many personal injury attorneys will outline these criteria in their contracts. For example, if they get a case settled before filing a lawsuit, the client will pay a certain percentage. However, the percentage increases if they go to litigation or reach a certain number of days within a trial.

On the client side, a nice thing about this method is that you do not have to worry about paying monthly bills or a retainer up front. Also, if you lose the case, you don't have to pay the attorney anything. You also don't have to pay any costs or expenses. They are fully covered. It's not uncommon for my office to spend $75,000 on expenses for a case. The client does not have to pay it until the end of the case, at which point they reimburse the attorney out of the settlement or judgment money the client receives.

Many people also have concerns about whether they will end up netting anything after paying attorney's fees. It is the policy of my practice, as well as most ethical attorneys I know, to decline cases in which the client would not net a significant amount after all expenses are accounted for. A case can settle for $1,000,000, but if there's $999,999 of attorney's fees, expenses, medical bills, and so forth, and the client only nets a dollar, the attorney did nothing to truly benefit the client in arguably the most challenging time of their life.

What Makes My Firm Different

I believe there are five key aspects of my legal practice that set my office apart from other personal injury attorneys...

1.) **Experience.** I am a genuine trial attorney. I don't just say this; I prove it. My track record demonstrates more trial experience than at least 90% of attorneys in the United States.

2.) **Insider Knowledge.** I have handled cases from both sides of the fence. Having worked for insurance companies in the past and having switched over to advocating for injured victims, my experience has given me a unique insight and edge. I know the playbook that the insurance companies have. I've not only studied it, but I've actively been a part of it.

3.) **Aggressiveness.** I fight for my clients from the heart. I believe in them and am ready to take anything on for them, including big, wealthy, and powerful insurance companies. When push comes to shove, I do not take on a case unless I am willing to go all the way and take it to trial. That is not to say I take every case to trial. Most cases do not go that far and end up in a settlement.

4.) **Compassion.** This may seem to contradict my second strength, but it does not. The compassion I have for my clients fuels the aggression with which I fight for them when the time comes. I truly believe the job of a personal injury attorney is not only to get the client the most money possible, but to get them the medical treatment needed so they can recover. Money is not worth the pain and suffering many experience due to an injury-inducing incident. My sense of compassion drives me to connect my clients with the right doctors – and find the best case outcome available – so they can *truly* make a full recovery.

5.) **Keen Litigation Skills.** Many attorneys I know, some of whom are personal injury attorneys, are not true litigators. They are not able, if willing at all, to go to court and fight the insurance companies. They take cases with the goal of working them up as quickly as possible to secure a settlement and move on to the next case. I even know an attorney that brags about how fast his average case settles. Insurance companies take advantage of these kinds of attorneys. I, on the other hand, am a fighter. I am a litigator.

CHAPTER SEVEN

CLOSING REMARKS

As I've stated many times in this book, personal injury law is a remarkably specialized field. The law is very complex, and you need to know what you're doing in order to navigate it effectively. There are a lot of landmines you can step on that can tank your case in a heartbeat, and simply having an attorney doesn't guarantee you avoid these landmines. You need one who truly knows what they're doing - you need a dedicated personal injury attorney.

Personal injury law has many nuances. Hiring a qualified personal injury attorney is the doorway to success. A qualified personal injury attorney will not only fight for you and take your case to trial, but they will also communicate with doctors, understand the medicine and the procedures, and guide you through the medical process to help your physical and emotional healing.

Insurance companies know which attorneys are willing to go to trial for their clients and which are not. While I was working for insurance companies, there was a personal injury law firm we dealt with often. We realized that they would never take a case to trial, so we were constantly intentionally trying to force them in that direction, as though it was all just a game. We purposefully lowballed our offers with the goal of directing the case toward trial, and they always took the bait – they settled every single case. Insurance companies pay attention to an attorney's track record, and their offers reflect it. Attorneys with a history and willingness to go to trial are more likely to get you more money, regardless of how the case actually ends.

This is also a major reason why getting an attorney involved in your case is vital, even if it appears as though it will be an obvious win due to clear liability. Partnering with a personal injury attorney means you do not need to deal with the stress and anxiety associated with the case or the insurance companies involved. Instead, you can focus on what matters most: healing. Moreover, a skilled personal injury attorney will drive the value of your case up, meaning you will receive more money than you could ever secure on your own.

What Is The Next Step?

As a husband-and-wife team, we understand how a serious injury can affect the entire family. Let us help you get the financial compensation you need to move forward. We do not collect a fee unless we win! Dial (833) GO-MEYER or visit www.meyerinjurylawyers.com to schedule a free consultation with our California or Idaho personal injury attorneys today.

INDEX

NOTES

Made in the USA
Monee, IL
05 November 2026

67387960R00052